A Dog Named
Ranger

Ann Ulrich Miller

Earth Star Publications

A Dog Named Ranger

Ann Ulrich Miller

EARTH STAR PUBLICATIONS
Pagosa Springs, Colorado

First Edition
First Printing November 2012

ISBN 978-0-944851-34-0

Printed in the United States of America

To Gary and Carol Dillard
in gratitude

And to Ethan
with fondest memories

December 2000

My life began when I was born at the Ferrier Ranch on January 30, 2000 — on Super Bowl Sunday. Now I have no idea what that means — Super Bowl Sunday.

Can anyone tell me — what is a "Super Bowl"? Why anyone would designate a *Sunday* in honor of a giant *drinking dish* is beyond me.

Anyway, I was one of several puppies born to my mother — a blue heeler, and my father — an Australian shepherd. My mom had never had a litter of puppies before. I don't think she knew what she was getting into.

It turns out she lost interest in us a week or so later. Her milk dried up, and Harry — the man who lived on the ranch outside Crawford, Colorado— had to feed us cow's milk to keep us alive.

My memories of those days on the Ferrier Ranch are vague. My first real memory is the day I went for a

ride in Harry's pickup truck. It was five weeks after I
was born — on March 5, 2000, to be exact — and
Harry had me wrapped up in an old blanket in the
front seat. He arrived at somebody's property across
the valley and he got out and took his tools out of the
back of the truck while I took a little nap.

After Harry's work was done, he reached into the
front seat and woke me up. He cradled me in his arms

and showed me to
a man and a
woman standing
outside next to
three mules that
were tied up next
to the barn.

The tall man
had white hair and
a beard and wore a
black cowboy hat and a green jacket. The smaller
woman standing next to him had curly reddish hair
and wore blue jeans and a denim jacket. They both
peered curiously at me as Harry slowly uncovered the
blanket to show them what I looked like.

The man chuckled. "Why, he looks like a baby
skunk." The men laughed and the woman reached her
hand over to caress me. I had black fur and a white
collar, but no tail. I *did* look like a skunk — at least in
the beginning.

"His mother rejected him," Harry told the couple. He explained my heritage and then said he had planned to give the pup — *me* — to a friend who wanted him. But when he got to the man's house, the wife had said no. He asked this man and woman if they wanted to give me a home.

The woman smiled and took me into her arms. "Oh, he's so cute," she said. Then she sighed as she glanced at the bearded man with the cowboy hat. "But I really don't think we're ready for a dog."

There was a short silence. I saw the look in the man's blue eyes and I saw the look in the small woman's green eyes. Then I heard her suddenly tell Harry, "Well ... I suppose we could give it a try."

Well, since that day in early March, I found my true parents. Ethan Miller was a devoted master and father to me. He kept me next to his bed at night — in a box — and he always woke up when I started to whimper. He would take me outside in the middle of the night to pee.

My mom, whose name was Annie, bragged to people that I never had to actually be "house trained" because I picked it up instinctively. She was very

proud of me.

They had to feed me milk for a while, and then I graduated to puppy chow. They named me Ranger.

"He is such a tiny little bundle of energy and cuteness," Annie would say. She would laugh at my antics. I knew I was intelligent and playful, but most importantly I knew that they loved me. And I gave that love back to them. I was a happy and healthy Australian shepherd/blue heeler puppy. My white mane gave me that collie look, and I had tick markings on my chest and legs.

Friends of Annie's and Ethan's, Mike and Laraine, got a kick out of me when I was a puppy. They had recently lost their beloved dog, Zeus, but didn't want to get another dog. I was so lovable and I liked everybody and expected everyone to love me as well. They usually did. There were a few exceptions ...

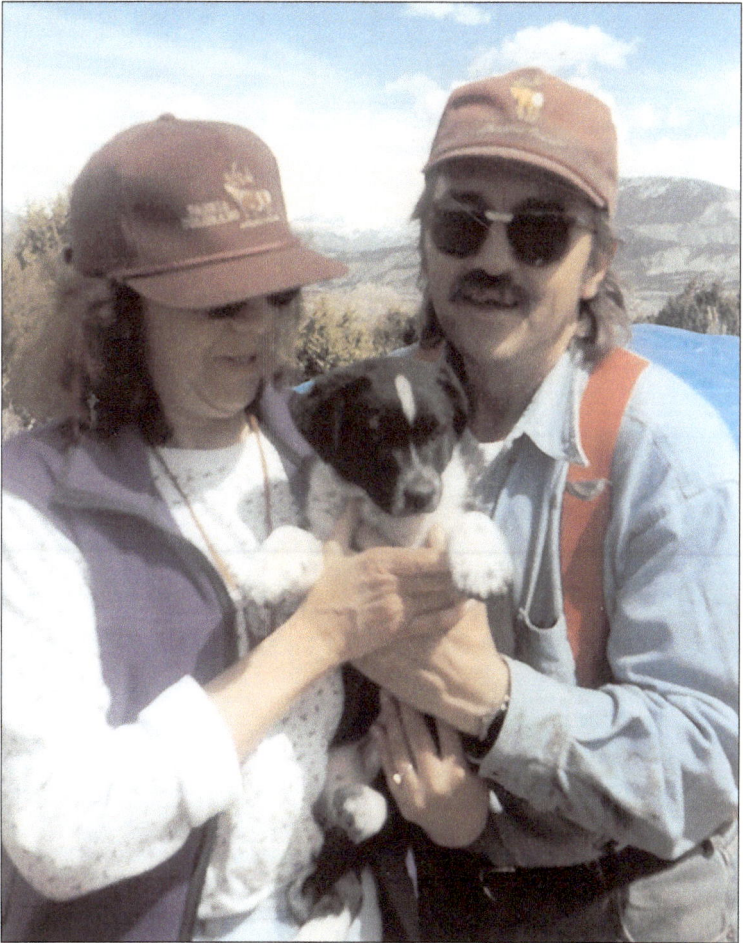

Laraine and Mike holding Ranger when he was a puppy

Annie's oldest son, Ryan, never quite got used to dogs. Ryan is a "cat person" and when he was growing up they had only cats — never any dogs. A few times in his childhood Ryan got chased by dogs, so he avoided them.

I only wanted to get Ryan to *like* me. I went after Ryan more than anyone else and just insisted that

Ryan was going to like me. I would jump up on him all of the time. The first time Ryan saw me was when he came home for the weekend and was on crutches for some injury either at work or college. Anyway, I'll never forget the expression on Ryan's face when I went charging at him when he was on those crutches.

Annie's other two sons, Marty and Scotty, were dog lovers and got along well with me. Marty came to live with us in September 2001. Scott had come the summer before — in 2000 — when I was still a pup. Everyone who came to our place got to know me.

I actually thought cats should automatically love me too. "Mu," the cat, who was starting to get old, was a ginger tabby. Mu was not pleased that a puppy had come into her life. It took the old girl a long time to get used to a dog in the house, and of course I wanted to play rough with her. She would have none of that. Eventually, though, we became friends and we were all one big happy family.

Mu, the Cat

Mu was a mighty hunter who liked to catch packrats and chew their heads off. Mu soon learned that I was fond of baby rabbits. Mu would hunt and catch a baby rabbit, then bring it to me. I would then pounce on it and gobble the whole thing down in one gulp.

Years later, "Jasmine," another cat, joined our family. Jasmine was Annie's mother's cat from Pahrump, Nevada — a real "fraidy cat," as I recall.

I was an active puppy and wanted to play all the time. I felt it was my purpose to show Ethan and Annie how to play and have fun. I loved to fetch sticks and chase balls. They found things for me to chew on.

Jasmine

Ethan took two empty plastic bottles and tied a thin rope between them. I would drag those bottles all around and twirl them through the air. It was my best toy. I would then run around, dragging the rope and bottles, and I'd swing it round and round. It would make them laugh. How I loved that sound.

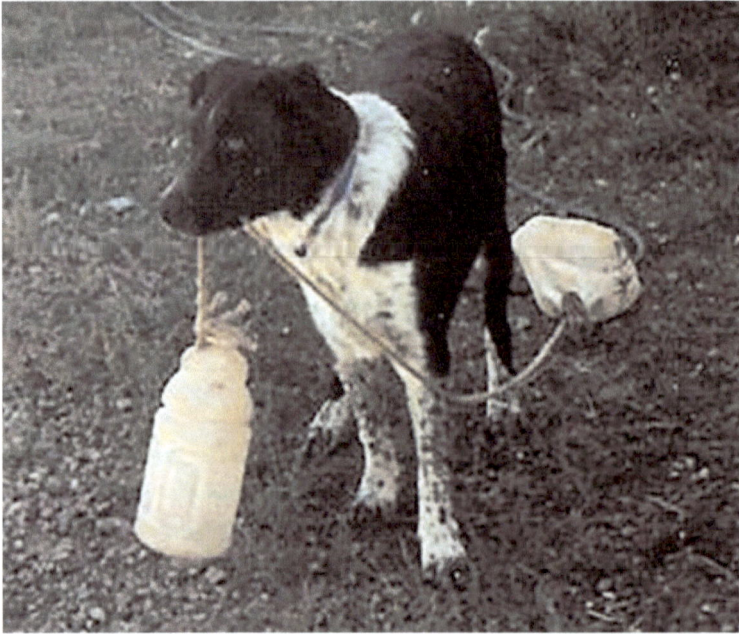

I found out why Ethan and Annie named our place the "Second Chance Ranch." It was because they specialized in giving everything on it a "second chance." Before that, Ethan and Annie had jokingly called it the "Reject Ranch," but then they decided that name was too negative.

It was true, just about everything and everyone on it was getting a second chance, including Ethan and

Annie. I had been rejected by my mother as a puppy, so they had given me a second chance. Even Mu and Jasmine had their second chance coming to live with them.

Ethan and Annie took me everywhere they went. I rode in the truck — inside a box at first. I loved to go places in the car. Annie took me to her work at the newspaper a few times and the people there gathered around me and laughed and said I was really cute.

I wasn't used to being on a leash, but if we were in town for any reason, Annie would leash me and I was so strong, I'd pull *her* along rather than the other way around.

Sometimes a dog comes into your life to show you that life should not be so serious. I taught my people to laugh and have a good time. Play was my greatest activity and I would go to extremes to show others how to do it.

I loved to fetch sticks. Unfortunately, one time when Ethan and Annie were up in the mountains camping, I chased after a stick in the woods and as I was bringing it back to them — just as fast as my legs would carry me — part of the stick caught the trunk of a tree. I whined and cringed in pain — the stick broke off one of my canine teeth.

When I played, I gave it everything I had. And being an Aussie dog, I was also intelligent. I picked up the English language by listening to Ethan. One time a friend of my dad's, named Ken Spencer, was over at our house visiting. Ken can read animals' minds, and he made a comment about me: "That dog has an *unusual* vocabulary!" There was mention about "four-letter words," but I don't know what the hell that means.

Ethan and Koko

The mules were big animals. They could have crushed me in one kick or mis-step. But I wasn't worried about that. I was a natural around the mules. In the beginning, Annie was scared to death that one of the mules would step on me or kick me because I would get so close — right under their feet sometimes. I had to learn to stay some distance away from those huge beasts.

Miranda was the biggest of the mules. She was a brown molly and had a gentle disposition. She was so laid back, anybody could ride her. Koko was strictly a pack mule. He was a handsome black john with white legs. He followed Miranda around like she was his mama.

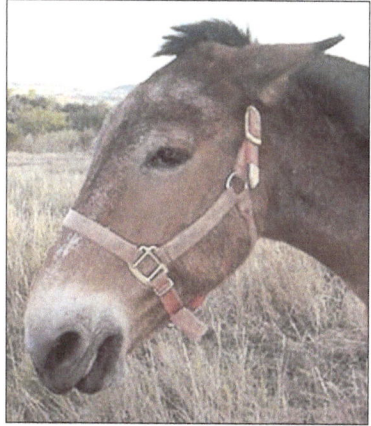

Miranda

Then there was Jenny, a gray molly who appeared to have some burro in her. Jenny was high-strung and unpredictable. She was supposed to be Annie's mule to ride, but I could tell Annie was afraid of Jenny.

We had an electric fence when we had the mules,

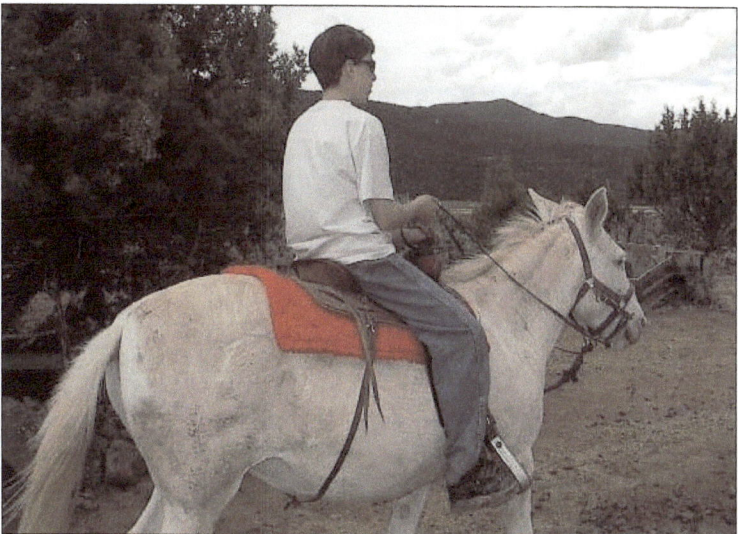

Scott riding Jenny

and when I was a puppy I got caught up in the electric fence at least two times that I know of. I soon learned to respect the fence and not go near it.

When Annie's youngest son Scott came to visit during my first summer on the Second Chance Ranch, he would ride Jenny. Scott took to

Ranger, Koko and Ethan

Scott with Ranger

the mules without any hesitation. He could handle Jenny and they would go on rides and he'd make her go *fast* — which she loved. I would bark and chase after them, but then Annie would get mad at me and sometimes close me up inside the house. She was still afraid I'd get trampled.

I was glad that Scott was on the ranch that

summer. I liked having a boy for a companion.

That summer was when Marcy came to Colorado and we became fast friends. Marcy came to visit at the Second Chance Ranch in early June, and she loved it so much that Ethan and Annie decided to help her move to Colorado all the way from Ohio. And it's a good thing she did, because Marcy was the one who baby-sat the pets whenever Ethan and Annie went on a trip. Marcy had a way with animals and she loved me.

When he drove the tractor, Ethan would put me inside one of his big coat pockets and we'd ride around the ranch. Soon I grew too big to do that, so I'd follow along on foot. Whenever Ethan worked on something, I was right there next to him.

When they watered the trees they had planted next to the house, I made a game out of chasing the hose. I liked to pretend the hose was a snake monster and attack it.

At first they laughed at me. This encouraged me to play harder at the game. But then they got mad at me for chewing on it. I didn't know any better. I didn't know that putting lots of holes in a hose with my sharp teeth makes it useless.

Then one day I discovered the shovel. That was the day when Ethan was digging near the house. I suddenly went berserk over the shovel. I barked and attacked the shovel as if it were alive. Annie went into hysterics laughing, and said it was the funniest thing she'd ever seen.

After that, she would throw the shovel out in the middle of the yard and I would take it over — barking, attacking, biting — even using my strong nose to push the tool up into the air.

I could spin it around and use the shovel like a gouging tool, sliding it across the driveway or the snow if it was winter. Then, afterwards, I would be so exhausted, I'd lie there panting, but happy after a good long workout with the shovel. From that day forward the shovel became my favorite game and gave us lots of thrills in the years to come.

Ethan and Annie raised some goslings for their mountain man friend, Neal, who lived out in the adobes near Orchard City. He had heard that geese made good "watch birds," so he paid for the geese and asked Ethan and Annie to raise them, since we already had accommodations for poultry.

Annie raised her first batch of chicks in the spring of 2000, and she kept chickens for many years to come. The geese were fun, but I wasn't allowed to chase them. They had to be kept in a

one of which was crippled.

Annie gave the lame turkey special love and attention, and "Precious" grew big and fat alongside the other turkeys.

It was my mission in life to help guard and protect Annie's birds. I was very good at rounding them up and herding them whenever it was needed. I would never hurt any of them. *Ever!*

I was — first and foremost — Ethan's dog.

separate fenced-in area apart from the chickens.

When Annie added turkeys to our menagerie, it came about because Mike and Laraine one day told Annie about some abandoned young turkeys. So she brought home four Bourbon reds and four bronze-breasted turkeys,

Man's Best Friend

We were true companions and spent all of our time together. Ethan referred to me as "Dog," even though my name is Ranger. They had other nicknames for me, which included "Woggins," "Boy" and "Ranger Danger."

When a thunderstorm happened, I did not like the crash of thunder. I would get very nervous and start panting and whining. I also didn't like gunfire. I would run if I heard the clap of a gunshot.

When winter came, I welcomed the snow. Another one of my favorite games was "playing snow-ball." Annie would form a snowball in her hands and then toss it up into the air, and I'd jump up and catch it in my mouth.

Ranger with Marty

That was so much fun, I just had to do it over and over again. Sometimes, though, it made my nose cold and my teeth tingle.

On my birthday each year — January 30 — Annie would bake me an angel food cake. Then she would place birthday candles in it and they'd sing to me. Then I would get my own piece of birthday cake.

But you know? No one ever mentioned that my birthday was on "Super Bowl Sunday" after that first year. I just have never been able to figure that out.

In fall of 2004, Ethan and Annie took a month-

On the road

long trip to Ohio, and they took me along. I loved long-distance travel and rode on the ledge behind Ethan's seat the whole way.

I played football with the boys when we visited Ethan's son Randy in Ravenna. They were tossing a football back and forth and I just couldn't help myself — I love balls! I *had* to be part of it.

Then, while we were visiting Ethan's brother Dale's farm in Somerset, Pennsylvania, I made friends with Dale's dog, "Juke," who was bigger than me. We two dog cousins had quite a time romping in the barnyard together. I felt very much at home there, mostly

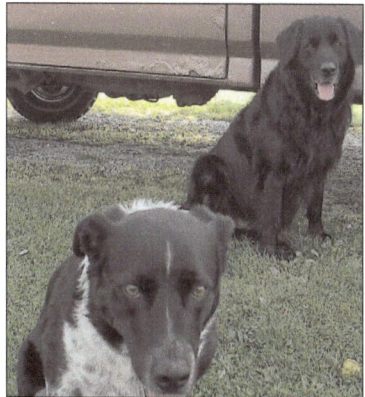
Dog cousins

because they had chickens.

A few days after we returned home to Colorado, there were a couple of episodes with the chickens. "Frances," one of Annie's hens, came up short in the night count. Annie worried all the next day about predators. There had been an attack on the turkeys by some wild animal during our trip to Ohio and two birds had been killed.

She was getting some feed out for the turkeys and kept the grain in metal cans with lids, right inside the barn. When she lifted the lid, *there* was Frances — and underneath her was a brown egg she had laid! Annie

had no idea how that chicken managed to jump in there without being seen, but she was relieved.

What were the chances of something like that happening twice in a week? The following weekend another chicken came up missing. Annie didn't know which one it was. It was evening and Annie and I had just checked the barn for stray eggs when I smelled something. So I began nosing around at an overturned rubber pail on the floor.

At first Annie tried to get me away from it. Then, curiosity got the better of her, so she carefully reached down and lifted up one side of the pail. There was one of her *brown pullets*. The young hen had gotten trapped under the overturned pail — and beside her was a small green egg! The pullet must have perched on the side of the pail and upset it. It then flipped over on top of her and she had spent the last day and a half *"im-pailed."*

Ethan and Ranger

L ife was good for many years. And then something happened. In February 2006 Ethan became ill. It was sudden. He and Annie and I had all been out hiking near the Fire Mountain ditch two days before. And now, suddenly, he couldn't breathe. Annie called the EMTs and then she drove Ethan to the hospital in Delta, and I went with them.

Ethan's coughing spells drained him. I had to wait in the car the whole time they were at the hospital, so Annie had to come out often and check on me. Finally, they let Ethan come home. The doctor ordered him to be on full-time oxygen. His lungs were not in good shape. And after that, we didn't play any more — at least not like we used to. It was a sad time for us all.

It was in the fall of that year that we took another long trip to Ohio. This time the oxygen concentrator machine took up a lot of space in the back seat of their white Chevy car. But I rode along beside it. I wasn't about to miss out on any long trips.

It was a sunny day on October 1, 2006, with blue sky and plenty of green lawns and forest in New Matamoras, Ohio. Ethan and Annie looked at a house in the country. The real estate lady didn't mind that I had come along. I was impressed by the size of the place and I loved the woods and wanted to go explore them.

After the showing, Ethan and Annie drove farther down Jackson Run and came out Archer's Fork so that they could see more of the national forest. They let me out to run a bit and to get a drink of "earth water" (*my favorite*) from the stream.

That night, after we got back to the motel in Marietta, they talked it over and decided to submit an offer for that property. Annie made an appointment to go in and draw up some papers the next day.

Jackson Run

It was on my birthday, January 30, 2007, that we moved to Ohio. Snow came to New Matamoras that next day when we arrived.

In the spring, Ethan's granddaughter Brandi was down visiting us with her parents, Ron and Jan.

Brandi would take the ATV out and drive it all over the field.

Brandi and Annie hiked into the woods and it was a good thing I was along because Annie had this tendency to lose her sense of direction, and I always knew the way home.

With the arrival of May, the trees on Jackson Run finally leafed out and the green-ness

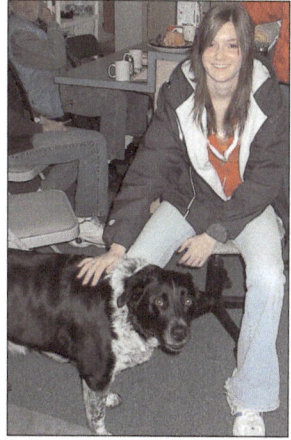

Ranger with Brandi

was all around us. The songbirds delighted us. Annie and I took more walks in the woods. Each time we ventured out, she grew more confident about not seeing any snakes. I have no idea why she worried about such things.

They planted a garden in the spring. A raccoon came around for the bird seed that fell onto the porch. I got excited about it. And once there was a 'possum that I barked at.

There were so many warblers and songbirds in that area that Annie said she was in bird heaven. We just couldn't get enough of nature.

Ever since we had to say goodbye to Jasmine and Mu, who had left us during that last year in Colorado, Annie had promised I could have a new kitty someday. We had to wait until we moved to Ohio, of course. Well, I had waited long enough.

On Saturday, July 21, 2007, Ron, Jan and Brandi visited us for the weekend. That was the day Ethan's niece Amy and her husband John Rohaley and their two girls brought us my new kitten. Amy brought us a black female with yellow eyes. They had named her "Clyde." I was ecstatic.

But when the new kitten was introduced to me

and saw that I was this big strange dog, her fur bristled up and her back and tail arched. She hissed at me and looked just like the classic Halloween cat!

I slunk off, my feelings deeply hurt because my new kitty didn't like me. We

Jessica, 3 months old

wondered how we were ever going to come to terms with each other. Annie liked having "matching pets" — a black kitty and a black-and-white dog.

Ethan named the new kitten "Jessica." We all thought it was the perfect name for her. None of us wanted to keep calling her Clyde, for heaven's sake. But we soon realized that "Clyde" was appropriate. Jessica as a kitten was extremely clumsy and had the habit of knocking things over, sometimes breaking them. "Clyde the Clod!" And that's how she eventually came to have the name: Jessica C. Miller — the C. stood for Clyde.

Jessica was always busy playing with something. She played hard and she slept hard. She established favorite sleeping spots around the house, which included on top of the refrigerator, beneath the coffee table, and a number of eccentric locations throughout the house, her favorite being the bathroom sinks and bath tubs.

Jessica napping in the sink

For the first month or so, they didn't let Jessica outside unless she was restrained. She had gotten away from Annie a couple of times and always shot up the trunks of the tall cedar trees next to the porch. Then she couldn't get down on her own and Annie would have to go get the ladder.

Eventually, though, Jessica held her ground and she pulled a couple of "all nighters" outside. When we realized she was still alive in the morning, Jessica was allowed to have occasional nights out. She soon developed her instinctual hunting skills. Unfortunately, there were no baby rabbits around for me to feast on.

In August 2007, Ryan and Trish came to live at our house for a month. Annie's son Ryan had married Trish Neal in July. They brought their two male cats, Peloquin and Hamlet, who got along well with Jessica and even came to tolerate me — the *dog*. Jessie liked having her "uncles" there to play with. She was a very sociable cat. Jessica had been with us only about three weeks by then. She and I finally got to be friends. When I'd startle her, she'd still hunch up her back and hiss at me in Halloween cat fashion. And I have to admit, I grew a little jealous of the attention they gave Jessica.

On the down side, Jessica had brought fleas to our house. In the fall she and I were both still scratching

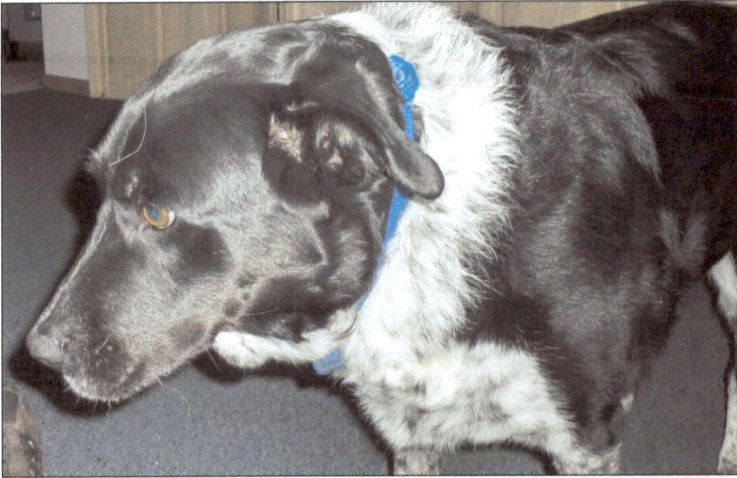

from them, but Annie gave us both some medicine each month. *Grrrrr*, how I hated having that stuff put on me. Eventually, though, the miserable fleas subsided.

The first week in December we got dumped with snow. Then I got sick from eating pork bones. I was constipated and miserable, so Ethan and Annie took me to the vet in New Martinsville, but the vet told them to take me immediately to the Parkersburg Veterinary Hospital, where they could x-ray me and do surgery, if necessary. Apparently, pork bones — or any bones, for that matter — are bad for dogs. This was *not what I wanted to hear!*

I had to stay overnight at the vet's, but I came home the next day. They gave me stool softener medication, but then on Thursday I grew worse. Thursday night was miserable and I kept my parents up, wanting to go outside a lot. I couldn't pass stool and I vomited some yellow-green liquid.

They took me back to Parkersburg the next day. I stayed overnight again and was given two enemas. A second x-ray showed that my colon was clear. From then on — much to my chagrin — they kept bones away from me.

Annie said that Jessica and I were hilarious at Christmas that year. Like two little kids, we were excited. I understood gifts and wanted to open mine. Both of us animals were in a festive, playful mood.

Annie opened my present from our friend Marcy in Colorado. It was a plastic football. Marcy had made

Jessica a catnip mouse. It was so cute to see Jessica playing with it.

I immediately chewed my football toy and tore a piece out of it, so they had to take it away. I felt so sad and betrayed. Then they decided I could open another present under the tree, so I got my large, glow-in-the-dark orange ball that I couldn't tear chunks out of. The rest of the presents had to wait for our belated Christmas with Annie's boys, who came on New Year's.

That New Year's was our last holiday together with Ethan. Annie's three sons — Ryan, Marty and Scott — were all there.

Ethan wasn't as chipper as he used to be. In fact, his health was getting worse. As the year progressed things went downhill. I stayed with him as much as I could, often just lying at his side either in the bedroom or as he watched television in the living room from his recliner.

I thought it was big fun when Annie served Ethan his meals in the bedroom ... sort of like a picnic. It was nice that they kept the patio curtains open. While lying in bed, Ethan could see the view of his backyard and all those green woods. I'm sure it had a healing effect on all of us.

August 2008 was a challenging month for us. Ethan had gone to the hospital for a week and was now home, but he couldn't do much of anything, and he had this chair on wheels that he sat in to move around the house. He no longer went outside.

One evening Annie and I took a few minutes at dusk and went for a quick walk down the road to the end of our property, then cut across our field to come home. Annie said that just those few minutes away from the house were helpful. She was busy taking care of Ethan and I could see that he tired her out.

Sometimes it felt like "death" in the house. I often felt the need to spend time outside, alone, on the porch. As for Annie, I noticed she usually tried to find excuses to do things in rooms where Ethan was not. Looking back now, it makes me really sad that she felt that way. But there was such a heaviness — the cloud of "doom" — hanging around my dad, and Annie found it unsettling.

I stayed close beside him. I knew that he wasn't

intentionally trying to drain her energy, but it was evident that her energy was being zapped.

Annie's brother Jim and his wife Linda came for a visit and they took a walk through the woods with me. Annie couldn't accompany us because of Ethan. They stayed only a couple of days, then left.

In early September Ron came down from Rootstown to take care of our dad so that Annie could fly to Colorado and meet her new grandson, Vorian. Ryan and Trish had a baby boy in July, and she badly

needed a break. Ron was close to Ethan and they had some really good father-and-son talks that week.

Then it was the day of September 12, 2008. Up till now I had accepted everything that was happening. I knew my dad was going away soon. Jessica also sensed that it was *the* day. She even jumped up on the bed before she went outside for the evening — something she *never* did — to say goodbye to her dad.

The Hospice nurse came and stayed with Annie throughout the evening. I stayed next to Ethan as he suffered through his last hours. When he went to the Other Place, we felt a sense of relief. Annie was sad, but she knew and was prepared for this moment — and we realized we would have to go on without him.

Three weeks later, some of Annie's family arrived for Ethan's memorial service, which was to be held in Somerset, Pennsylvania, where my dad was born. Annie put heat on in the travel trailer and she slept out there because she had a house full of company. On Saturday morning she got up and made a pancake breakfast for everyone and then we headed over to Pennsylvania in two cars. I stayed with Annie and the boys in a pet-friendly motel.

During the service I had to stay in the car. The minister didn't allow dogs in his church. But

Saying goodbye

afterwards we drove to the cemetery and Annie left Ethan's ashes there to be buried in his plot. I will never forget that day with all those people who knew and loved Ethan.

For months I was sad. Often I simply laid around, moping and missing Ethan.

At Christmastime Annie took me to Montgomery, Alabama, to spend the holidays with Scotty. I got to meet Scott's cat, "Domino," and for the first time in my life I got my toes wet in the ocean at Gulf Breeze, Fla.

And then one day, in the spring, change came. Annie had a great big garage sale, and then she began packing boxes with all our things.

One day she loaded up the back of the Windstar with some of her chickens and we took a trip to

Wisconsin. She gave her rooster and some of her favorite hens to her niece, who lived in the country. Then we visited her other relatives and I got to meet more dog cousins in Madison, including Keegan, the Corgi, and his two pals, Sadie and Gonzo.

Not long after we returned to Jackson Run, a big moving van arrived and they loaded up everything we owned. Annie told me we were moving back to Colorado. I was going *home*.

For three days, Jessica and I rode in the car with Annie and her friend from Colorado who had come to help us move. It was on May 9, 2009 when we moved into the stucco house on Sundown Circle in Pagosa Springs.

I loved that house. It was roomy and it had a fenced-in yard with plenty of space to run. Jessica liked it too — especially all the pine siskins that lived in the

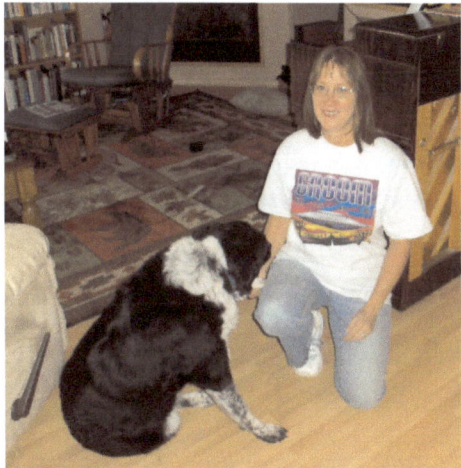

Ponderosas in the front yard. Jessica mastered the "doggy doors" right away.

I hate to admit this, but it took me several tries before I finally figured out how to go in and out of those flapping doors. But once I got it, I saw the benefit of it. I no longer had to wait and rely on Annie to let me in and out of the house whenever I wanted.

Everything was going along fine, but then Annie started going places without me. I was alone for hours at a time — and I did not like it one bit. I had been used to being with Ethan all of the time. We were practically inseparable all those years. Now it was different. I was lonely and I was concerned about Annie. Where was she? Was she all right?

Then I found out where she was most of the time. She had a new friend — a man — and she was over at his house a lot — sometimes overnight. I was not allowed to go over there, and that bothered me. After all, she was my mom — she needed to be home — with *me*.

I tried very hard to make that man like me, but Annie told me I couldn't go near him because he was "allergic" to dogs and cats. I didn't know what that word meant — *allergic*. And as time progressed, I grew more and more uneasy.

Finally, in February 2010, I met Gary and Carol, two of the most trusting people I've ever known. They came to our house and they petted me and they seemed like very nice people. They told Annie they had been looking for a dog like me for many years. They wanted to take me home.

But first they wanted me to get used to them. So they started coming every few days, and we'd go on a walk together. I really was starting to like being with Gary and Carol.

At the end of February, Annie drove me in the car up to Gary's and Carol's house on the hill. It was easier saying goodbye to Annie than I thought it would be, although she did end up staying the better part of an hour, to help me adjust to my new house.

It was the most beautiful place! They lived in the woods, on a hill on 50 acres, with a two-story stucco home. I was the only dog with a couple of cats, and in a few weeks they took me on a trip to Texas. I was afraid I was going to have a hard time emotionally, but it was more fun than anything else.

Gary and Carol gave me a loving home when I needed it most. I was 10 years old when I went to live with them, and I had occasional visits from Annie in my remaining three years. She could see that I was happy and adjusted to my new life with my wonderful new parents. And after 13 ½ years, it was time for me to go and be with Ethan again.

I got sick in September after Gary and I got home from visiting his mother in Texas, where I had spent some time. The vet, Polly, came to see me a lot. They gave me special food and medicine that only seemed to make me sicker. As my memory began to fail, I could only see and feel the great sadness in Gary's and Carol's faces. I did not want them to be sad. The time comes when all of us must leave.

On September 16, 2012, Annie dropped over to see me. She hadn't seen me in over a year. I didn't remember her because of my dementia, but I loved how she sat beside me and petted me for more than an hour while she and Gary talked quietly. She watched as he fed me soft food through a plunger and she saw how feeble I had become in my last days.

On Friday, September 21, I was finally able to stand up and walk outside. I was still weak, but I wanted to enjoy the beautiful Colorado sunshine and lie in my favorite spot in the woods, basking in the beauty I had grown to love. The next evening, on September 22, is when Polly came and she helped me go to the Other Place.

I am there now. I am happy. I am with Ethan, and I have brushed noses with my old friends, Mu and Jasmine. I have a young, healthy body again, much like I had when I was that roly-poly puppy that looked like a skunk when I arrived in Harry Ferrier's pickup truck on that day in early March.

Please don't be sad because I am not with you. I had a good life, lots of adventures, *lots of play!* I had people who loved me and I did a lot of things and went a lot of places. I smelled a lot of good smells. Think of me as I was — playful, happy and the best canine shovel juggler that ever lived.

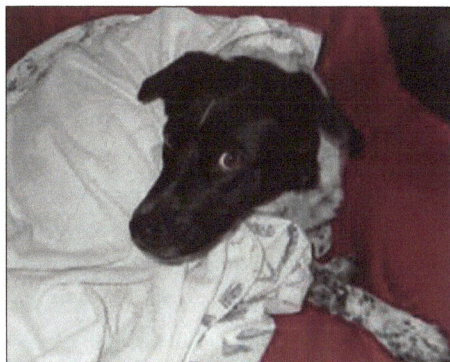

"If you could read my mind..."

Below: **"Uh-oh... I think they're home..."**

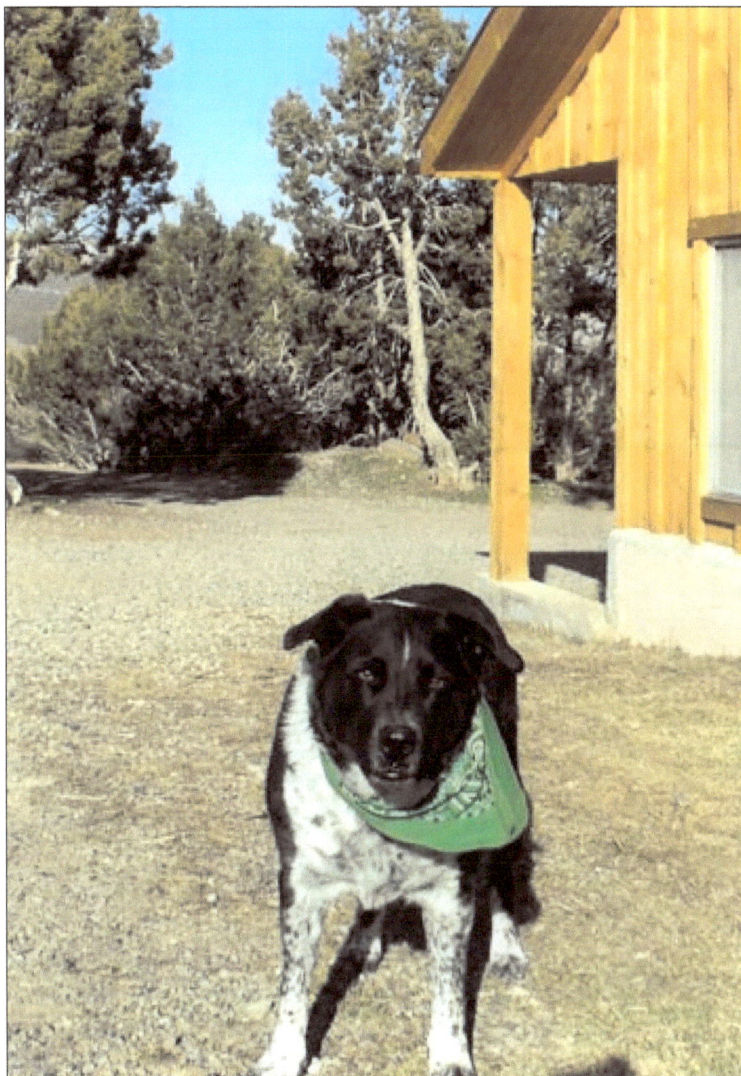

March 2006 on Stucker Mesa

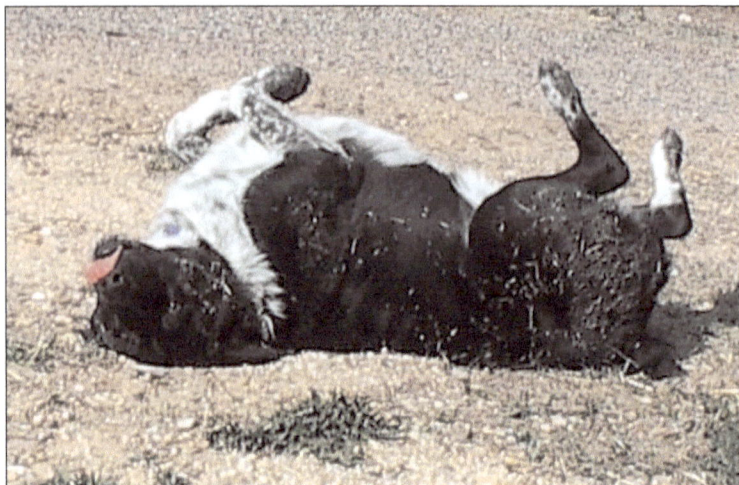

A good old canine-fashion back rub

Below: **Visiting Vorian in La Jara, Summer 2009**

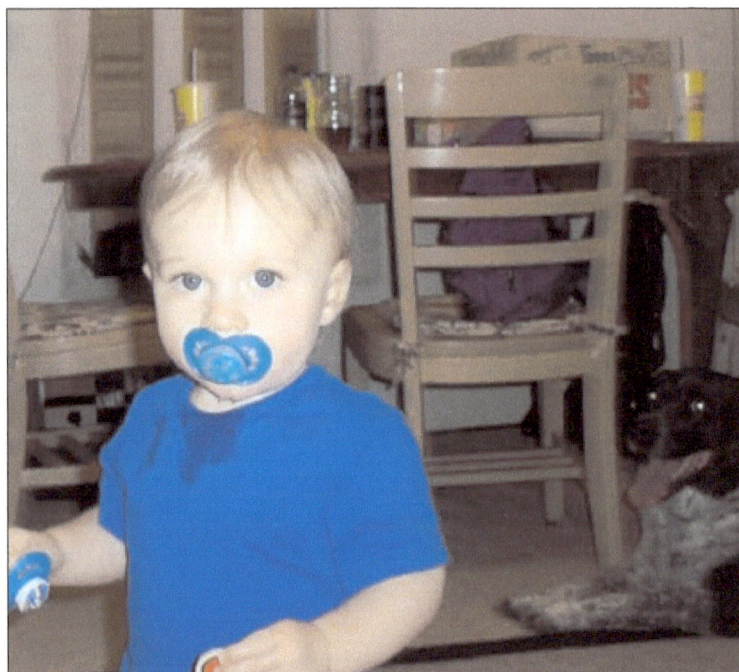

Ranger catching snowballs on Stucker Mesa

Below: **Scott and Ranger fishing on Stevens Gulch**

Marty and Ranger on Stucker Mesa

Below: **Ranger and Jessica**

Ranger running free on Stucker Mesa

Below: **Snow dog**

Ranger in his 13 ½ years enriched many people's lives. He will always be remembered and loved by all of us.

Earth Star Publications
216 Sundown Circle
Pagosa Springs, Colorado

www.earthstarpublications.com